SELECTIONS

FROM

The Hymnal 1982

IN LARGE PRINT

Church Publishing Incorporated
19 East 34th Street
New York, New York 10016
www.churchpublishing.org

PREFACE

Music has always played an important part in Anglican worship and in the individual spiritual lives of our people. This is especially true of older members of the Church who often find the words of a familiar hymn coming back to them at some crucial time in their lives. Those of us who have spent time leading worship in nursing homes and extended-care facilities know this very well.

Despite the rich resource we have in *The Hymnal 1982,* there are severe limitations for frail elderly in the weight of that book and the small print that eludes failing eyes. Also, as worship leaders, we do not find it easy to carry a stack of hymnals with us in our visits to facilities for the elderly. Many of us have produced our own booklets with less than satisfactory results and the possible infringement of copyright laws.

We are pleased that, through a cooperative effort of Church Publishing Incorporated and the Episcopal Society for Ministry on Aging, Inc. (ESMA), we have been able to produce a lightweight hymnal with large print and a thoughtful selection of familiar hymns for worship use in hospitals or homes. It is our hope that this book will make it easier for clergy and lay leaders to enrich the worship of those who are unable through age or disability to attend worship in their parish churches.

Of course no selection of hymns will satisfy everyone's taste. If your favorite hymn is missing, we apologize and ask that you forgive our oversight, caused in part because of the limit in size we have set for ourselves. Four other considerations influenced our choices: We wanted (1) hymns that have been in common use in the Episcopal Church for twenty-five years or more, (2) hymns with familiar melodies that are easy to sing, (3) some seasonal hymns, especially for Christmas and Easter, and (4) hymns that address some spiritual issues of older persons.

We hope that this book will be a useful resource for worship throughout the Church, knowing that "those who sing pray twice."

The Rev. Robert W. Carlson, D. Min.
President of the Board of Directors
Episcopal Society for Ministry on Aging
The Rev. Mary Martha Solbak, Deacon
Vice President, ESMA Board of Directors

Morning has broken 8

1 Morning has broken
like the first morning,
blackbird has spoken
like the first bird.
Praise for the singing!
Praise for the morning!
Praise for them, springing!
fresh from the Word!

2 Sweet the rain's new fall
sunlit from heaven,
like the first dewfall
on the first grass.
Praise for the sweetness
of the wet garden,
sprung in completeness
where his feet pass.

3 Mine is the sunlight!
Mine is the morning
born of the one light
Eden saw play!
Praise with elation,
praise every morning,
God's re-creation
of the new day!

Eleanor Farjeon (1881-1965), alt.

O come, O come, Emmanuel 56

1 O come, O come, Emmanuel,
and ransom captive Israel,
that mourns in lonely exile here
until the Son of God appear.

Rejoice! Rejoice! Emmanuel
shall come to thee, O Israel!

2 O come, thou Wisdom from on high,
who orderest all things mightily;
to us the path of knowledge show,
and teach us in her ways to go.

Refrain

3 O come, O come, thou Lord of might,
who to thy tribes on Sinai's height
in ancient times didst give the law,
in cloud, and majesty, and awe.

Refrain

4 O come, thou Branch of Jesse's tree,
free them from Satan's tyranny
that trust thy mighty power to save,
and give them victory o'er the grave.

Refrain

5 O come, thou Key of David, come,
and open wide our heavenly home;
make safe the way that leads on high,
and close the path to misery.

Rejoice! Rejoice! Emmanuel
shall come to thee, O Israel!

6 O come, thou Dayspring from on high,
and cheer us by thy drawing nigh;
disperse the gloomy clouds of night,
and death's dark shadow put to flight.

Refrain

7 O come, Desire of nations, bind
in one the hearts of all mankind;
bid thou our sad divisions cease,
and be thyself our King of Peace.

Refrain

8 O come, O come, Emmanuel,
and ransom captive Israel,
that mourns in lonely exile here
until the Son of God appear.

Refrain

Hymnal version, 1940, alt.;
based on Latin, ca. 9th cent.; sts. 1, 3-6, pub. Cologne, 1710

Sleepers, wake! 61

1 "Sleepers, wake!" A voice astounds us,
the shout of rampart guards surrounds us:
"Awake, Jerusalem, arise!"
Midnight's peace their cry has broken,
their urgent summons clearly spoken:
"The time has come, O maidens wise!
Rise up, and give us light;
the Bridegroom is in sight.
Alleluia!
Your lamps prepare
and hasten there,
that you the wedding feast
may share."

2 Zion hears the watchmen singing;
her heart with joyful hope is springing,
she wakes and hurries
through the night.
Forth he comes, her Bridegroom glorious
in strength of grace, in truth victorious:
her star is risen, her light grows bright.
Now come, most worthy Lord,
God's Son, Incarnate Word,
Alleluia!
We follow all
and heed your call
to come into the banquet hall.

3 Lamb of God, the heavens adore you;
let saints and angels sing before you,
as harps and cymbals
swell the sound.
Twelve great pearls, the city's portals:
through them we stream
to join the immortals
as we with joy your throne surround.

No eye has known the sight,
no ear heard such delight:
Alleluia!
Therefore we sing
to greet our King;
for ever let our praises ring.

Philip Nicolai (1556-1608); tr.
Carl P. Daw, Jr. (b. 1944) and others

Come, thou long-expected Jesus 66

1 Come, thou long-expected Jesus,
born to set thy people free;
from our fears and sins release us,
let us find our rest in thee.

2 Israel's strength and consolation,
hope of all the earth thou art:
dear desire of every nation,
joy of every longing heart.

3 Born thy people to deliver,
born a child, and yet a king,
born to reign in us for ever,
now thy gracious kingdom bring.

4 By thine own eternal Spirit
  rule in all our hearts alone;
by thine all-sufficient merit
  raise us to thy glorious throne.

Charles Wesley (1707-1788)

The King shall come 73

1 The King shall come when morning dawns
  and light triumphant breaks;
when beauty gilds the eastern hills
  and life to joy awakes.

2 Not, as of old, a little child,
  to bear, and fight, and die,
but crowned with glory like the sun
  that lights the morning sky.

3 The King shall come when morning dawns
  and earth's dark night is past;
O haste the rising of that morn,
  the day that e'er shall last;

4 and let the endless bliss begin,
by weary saints foretold,
when right shall triumph over wrong,
and truth shall be extolled.

5 The King shall come when morning dawns
and light and beauty brings:
Hail, Christ the Lord! Thy people pray,
come quickly, King of kings.

Greek; tr. John Brownlie (1859-1925), alt.

On Jordan's bank 76

1 On Jordan's bank the Baptist's cry
announces that the Lord is nigh;
awake and hearken, for he brings
glad tidings of the King of kings.

2 Then cleansed be every breast from sin;
make straight the way for God within,
and let each heart prepare a home
where such a mighty guest may come.

3 For thou art our salvation, Lord,
our refuge, and our great reward;
without thy grace we waste away
like flowers that wither and decay.

4 To heal the sick stretch out thine hand,
and bid the fallen sinner stand;
shine forth, and let thy light restore
earth's own true loveliness once more.

5 All praise, eternal Son, to thee,
whose advent doth thy people free;
whom with the Father we adore
and Holy Spirit evermore.

Charles Coffin (1676-1749);
tr. John Chandler (1806-1876), alt.

O little town of Bethlehem 79

1 O little town of Bethlehem,
how still we see thee lie!
Above thy deep and dreamless sleep
the silent stars go by;
yet in thy dark streets shineth
the everlasting Light;
the hopes and fears of all the years
are met in thee tonight.

2 For Christ is born of Mary;
and gathered all above,
while mortals sleep, the angels keep
their watch of wondering love.
O morning stars, together
proclaim the holy birth!
and praises sing to God the King,
and peace to men on earth.

3 How silently, how silently,
the wondrous gift is given!
So God imparts to human hearts
the blessings of his heaven.
No ear may hear his coming,
but in this world of sin,
where meek souls will receive him, still
the dear Christ enters in.

*4 Where children pure and happy
pray to the blessed Child,
where misery cries out to thee,
Son of the mother mild;
where charity stands watching
and faith holds wide the door,
the dark night wakes, the glory breaks,
and Christmas comes once more.

5 O holy Child of Bethlehem,
descend to us, we pray;
cast out our sin and enter in,
be born in us today.
We hear the Christmas angels
the great glad tidings tell;
O come to us, abide with us,
our Lord Emmanuel!

Phillips Brooks (1835-1893)

O come, all ye faithful 83

1 O come, all ye faithful,
joyful and triumphant,
O come ye, O come ye to Bethlehem;
come, and behold him,
born the King of angels;

O come, let us adore him,
Christ the Lord.

2 God from God,
Light from Light eternal,
lo! he abhors not the Virgin's womb;
only-begotten
Son of God the Father;

Refrain

3 Sing, choirs of angels,
sing in exultation,
sing, all ye citizens of heaven above;
glory to God,
glory in the highest;

Refrain

*4 See how the shepherds,
summoned to his cradle,
leaving their flocks, draw nigh to gaze;
we too will thither
bend our joyful footsteps;

O come, let us adore him,
Christ the Lord.

*5 Child, for us sinners
poor and in the manger,
we would embrace thee,
with love and awe;
who would not love thee,
loving us so dearly?

Refrain

6 Yea, Lord, we greet thee,
born this happy morning;
Jesus, to thee be glory given;
Word of the Father,
now in flesh appearing;

Refrain

John Francis Wade (1711-1786);
tr. Frederick Oakeley (1802-1880) and others

Hark! the herald angels sing 87

1 Hark! the herald angels sing
glory to the newborn King!
Peace on earth and mercy mild,
God and sinners reconciled!
Joyful, all ye nations, rise,
join the triumph of the skies;
with the angelic host proclaim
Christ is born in Bethlehem!

Hark! the herald angels sing
glory to the newborn King!

2 Christ, by highest heaven adored;
Christ, the everlasting Lord;
late in time behold him come,
offspring of the Virgin's womb.
Veiled in flesh the Godhead see;
hail the incarnate Deity.
Pleased as man with man to dwell;
Jesus, our Emmanuel!

Refrain

3 Mild he lays his glory by,
born that we no more may die,
born to raise us from the earth,
born to give us second birth.
Risen with healing in his wings,
light and life to all he brings,
hail, the Sun of Righteousness!
hail, the heaven-born Prince of Peace!

Hark! the herald angels sing
glory to the newborn King!

Charles Wesley (1707-1788), alt.

It came upon the midnight clear 89

1 It came upon the midnight clear,
that glorious song of old,
from angels bending near the earth
to touch their harps of gold:
"Peace on the earth, good will to men,
from heaven's all-gracious King."
The world in solemn stillness lay
to hear the angels sing.

2 Still through the cloven skies they come
with peaceful wings unfurled,
and still their heavenly music floats
o'er all the weary world;
above its sad and lowly plains
they bend on hovering wing,
and ever o'er its Babel-sounds
the blessed angels sing.

3 Yet with the woes of sin and strife
the world has suffered long;
beneath the heavenly hymn have rolled
two thousand years of wrong;
and warring humankind hears not
the tidings which they bring;
O hush the noise and cease your strife
and hear the angels sing!

4 For lo! the days are hastening on,
by prophets seen of old,
when with the ever-circling years
shall come the time foretold,
when peace shall over all the earth
its ancient splendors fling,
and all the world give back the song
which now the angels sing.

Edmund H. Sears (1810-1876), alt.

Angels we have heard on high 96

1 Angels we have heard on high,
singing sweetly through the night,
and the mountains in reply
echoing their brave delight.
Gloria in excelsis Deo.

2 Shepherds, why this jubilee?
Why these songs of happy cheer?
What great brightness did you see?
What glad tidings did you hear?
Gloria in excelsis Deo.

3 Come to Bethlehem and see
him whose birth the angels sing;
come, adore on bended knee
Christ, the Lord, the newborn King.
Gloria in excelsis Deo.

4 See him in a manger laid
whom the angels praise above;
Mary, Joseph, lend your aid,
while we raise our hearts in love.
Gloria in excelsis Deo.

French carol, alt. by Earl Marlatt (b. 1892)

Go tell it on the mountain 99

Refrain Go tell it on the mountain,
over the hills and everywhere;
go tell it on the mountain,
that Jesus Christ is born!

1 While shepherds kept their watching
o'er silent flocks by night,
behold, throughout the heavens
there shone a holy light.

Refrain

2 The shepherds feared and trembled
when lo! above the earth
rang out the angel chorus
that hailed our Savior's birth.

Refrain

3 Down in a lowly manger
the humble Christ was born,
and God sent us salvation
that blessed Christmas morn.

Refrain

Anonymous American folk hymn, 19th cent.;
adapt. John W. Work (b. 1901)

Joy to the world! 100

1 Joy to the world! the Lord is come:
let earth receive her King;
let every heart prepare him room,
and heaven and nature sing,

2 Joy to the world! the Savior reigns;
let us our songs employ,
while fields and floods,
rocks, hills and plains,
repeat the sounding joy.

*3 No more let sins and sorrows grow,
nor thorns infest the ground;
he comes to make his blessings flow
far as the curse is found.

4 He rules the world with truth and grace,
and makes the nations prove
the glories of his righteousness,
and wonders of his love.

Isaac Watts (1674-1748), alt.

Away in a manger 101

1 Away in a manger, no crib for his bed,
the little Lord Jesus
laid down his sweet head.
The stars in the bright sky
looked down where he lay,
the little Lord Jesus asleep on the hay.

2 The cattle are lowing, the baby awakes,
but little Lord Jesus
no crying he makes.
I love thee, Lord Jesus!
Look down from the sky,
and stay by my side until morning is nigh.

*3 Be near me, Lord Jesus; I ask thee to stay
close by me for ever, and love me I pray.
Bless all the dear children
in thy tender care,
and fit us for heaven
to live with thee there.

Traditional carol

God rest you merry, gentlemen 105

1 God rest you merry, gentlemen,
let nothing you dismay;
remember Christ our Savior
was born on Christmas Day,
to save us all from Satan's power
when we were gone astray.

O tidings of comfort and joy,
comfort and joy;
O tidings of comfort and joy!

2 From God our heavenly Father
a blessed angel came
and unto certain shepherds
brought tidings of the same:
how that in Bethlehem was born
the Son of God by name.

Refrain

3 “Fear not, then,” said the angel,
“Let nothing you affright;
this day is born a Savior
of a pure virgin bright,
to free all those who trust in him
from Satan’s power and might.”

O tidings of comfort and joy,
comfort and joy;
O tidings of comfort and joy!

4 Now to the Lord sing praises,
all you within this place,
and with true love and charity
each other now embrace;
this holy tide of Christmas
doth bring redeeming grace.

Refrain

London carol, 18th cent.
Words: By permission of Fleming H. Revell Company.

Good Christian friends, rejoice 107

1 Good Christian friends, rejoice
with heart and soul and voice;
give ye heed to what we say:
Jesus Christ is born today;
ox and ass before him bow,
and he is in the manger now.
Christ is born today!

2 Good Christian friends, rejoice
with heart and soul and voice;
now ye hear of endless bliss;
Jesus Christ was born for this!
He hath opened heaven's door,
and we are blest for evermore.
Christ was born for this!

3 Good Christian friends, rejoice
with heart and soul and voice;
now ye need not fear the grave:
Jesus Christ was born to save!
Calls you one and calls you all
to gain his everlasting hall.
Christ was born to save!

John Mason Neale (1818-1866), alt.

The first Nowell 109

1 The first Nowell the angel did say
was to certain poor shepherds in fields
as they lay;
in fields as they lay, keeping their sheep,
on a cold winter's night that was so deep.

Nowell, Nowell, Nowell, Nowell,
born is the King of Israel.

2 They looked up and saw a star
shining in the east beyond them far,
and to the earth it gave great light,
and so it continued both day and night.

Refrain

3 And by the light of that same star
three wise men came from country far;
to seek for a king was their intent,
and to follow the star wherever it went.

Refrain

*4 This star drew nigh to the northwest,
o'er Bethlehem it took its rest,
and there it did both stop and stay
right over the place where Jesus lay.

Refrain

*5 Then entered in those wise men three
full reverently upon their knee,
and offered there in his presence
their gold, and myrrh, and frankincense.

Refrain

6 Then let us all with one accord
sing praises to our heavenly Lord;
that hath made heaven
and earth of nought,
and with his blood our life hath bought.

Refrain

Old English Carol

Silent night, holy night 111

1 Silent night, holy night,
all is calm, all is bright
round yon virgin mother and child.
Holy infant, so tender and mild,
sleep in heavenly peace.

2 Silent night, holy night,
shepherds quake at the sight,
glories stream from heaven afar,
heavenly hosts sing alleluia;
Christ, the Savior, is born!

3 Silent night, holy night,
Son of God, love's pure light
radiant beams from thy holy face,
with the dawn of redeeming grace,
Jesus, Lord, at thy birth.

Joseph Mohr (1792-1848); tr. traditional

As with gladness men of old 119

1 As with gladness men of old
did the guiding star behold;
as with joy they hailed its light,
leading onward, beaming bright;
so, most gracious Lord, may we
evermore be led to thee.

2 As with joyful steps they sped
to that lowly manger-bed;
there to bend the knee before
him whom heaven and earth adore;
so may we with willing feet
ever seek the mercy-seat.

3 As they offered gifts most rare
at that manger rude and bare;
so may we with holy joy,
pure and free from sin's alloy,
all our costliest treasures bring,
Christ! to thee, our heavenly King.

4 Holy Jesus! every day
keep us in the narrow way;
and, when earthly things are past,
bring our ransomed souls at last
where they need no star to guide,
where no clouds thy glory hide.

5 In the heavenly country bright,
need they no created light;
thou its light, its joy, its crown,
thou its sun which goes not down:
there for ever may we sing
alleluias to our King.

William Chatterton Dix (1837-1898)

Alleluia, song of gladness 123

1 Alleluia, song of gladness,
voice of joy that cannot die;
alleluia is the anthem
ever raised by choirs on high;
in the house of God abiding
thus they sing eternally.

2 Alleluia thou resoundest,
true Jerusalem and free;
alleluia, joyful mother,
all thy children sing with thee;
but by Babylon's sad waters
mourning exiles now are we.

3 Alleluia though we cherish
and would chant for evermore
alleluia in our singing,
let us for a while give o'er,
as our Savior in his fasting
pleasures of the world forbore.

4 Therefore in our hymns we pray thee,
grant us, blessed Trinity,
at the last to keep thine Easter
with thy faithful saints on high;
there to thee for ever singing
alleluia joyfully.

Latin, llth cent.; tr. John Mason Neale (1818-1866), alt.

Songs of thankfulness 135

1 Songs of thankfulness and praise,
Jesus, Lord, to thee we raise,
Manifested by the star
to the sages from afar;
branch of royal David's stem
in thy birth at Bethlehem;
anthems be to thee addressed,
God in man made manifest.

2 Manifest at Jordan's stream,
Prophet, Priest, and King supreme;
and at Cana, wedding-guest,
in thy Godhead manifest;
manifest in power divine,
changing water into wine;
anthems be to thee addressed,
God in man made manifest.

3 Manifest in making whole
palsied limbs and fainting soul;
manifest in valiant fight,
quelling all the devil's might;
manifest in gracious will,
ever bringing good from ill;
anthems be to thee addressed,
God in man made manifest.

4 Manifest on mountain height,
shining in resplendent light,
where disciples filled with awe
thy transfigured glory saw.
When from there thou leddest them
steadfast to Jerusalem,
cross and Easter Day attest
God in man made manifest.

Sts. 1-3, Christopher Wordsworth (1807-1885)
St. 4, F. Bland Tucker (1895-1984)

Forty days and forty nights 150

1 Forty days and forty nights
thou wast fasting in the wild;
forty days and forty nights
tempted, and yet undefiled.

2 Should not we thy sorrow share
and from worldly joys abstain,
fasting with unceasing prayer,
strong with thee to suffer pain?

3 Then if Satan on us press,
Jesus, Savior, hear our call!
Victor in the wilderness,
grant we may not faint nor fall!

4 So shall we have peace divine:
holier gladness ours shall be;
round us, too, shall angels shine,
such as ministered to thee.

5 Keep, O keep us, Savior dear,
ever constant by thy side;
that with thee we may appear
at the eternal Eastertide.

George Hunt Smyttan (1822-1870), alt.

Welcome, happy morning! 179

1 "Welcome, happy morning!"
age to age shall say:
hell today is vanquished,
heaven is won today!
Lo! the dead is living, God for evermore!
Him their true Creator, all his works adore!
"Welcome, happy morning!"
age to age shall say.

*2 Earth her joy confesses,
clothing her for spring,
all fresh gifts returned
with her returning King:
bloom in every meadow,
leaves on every bough,
speak his sorrow ended,
hail his triumph now.
"Welcome, happy morning!"
age to age shall say.

*3 Months in due succession,
days of lengthening light,
hours and passing moments
praise thee in their flight.
Brightness of the morning,
sky and fields and sea,
Vanquisher of darkness,
bring their praise to thee.
"Welcome, happy morning!"
age to age shall say.

4 Maker and Redeemer,
life and health of all,
thou from heaven beholding
human nature's fall,
of the Father's Godhead
true and only Son,
mankind to deliver, manhood didst put on.
"Welcome, happy morning!"
age to age shall say.

5 Thou, of life the author,
death didst undergo,
tread the path of darkness,
saving strength to show;
come then, true and faithful,
now fulfill thy word,
'tis thine own third morning!
rise, O buried Lord!
"Welcome, happy morning!"
age to age shall say.

6 Loose the souls long prisoned,
bound with Satan's chain;
all that now is fallen raise to life again;
show thy face in brightness,
bid the nations see;
bring again our daylight:
day returns with thee!
"Welcome, happy morning!"
age to age shall say.

Venantius Honorius Fortunatus (540?-600?);
tr. John Ellerton (1826-1893), alt.

He is risen, he is risen! 180

1 He is risen, he is risen!
   Tell it out with joyful voice:
he has burst his three days' prison;
   let the whole wide earth rejoice:
death is conquered, we are free,
Christ has won the victory.

2 Come, ye sad and fearful-hearted,
   with glad smile and radiant brow!
Death's long shadows have departed;
   Jesus' woes are over now,
and the passion that he bore
sin and pain can vex no more.

*3 Come, with high and holy hymning,
   hail our Lord's triumphant day;
not one darksome cloud is dimming
   yonder glorious morning ray,
breaking o'er the purple east,
symbol of our Easter feast.

4 He is risen, he is risen!
He hath opened heaven's gate:
we are free from sin's dark prison,
risen to a holier state;
and a brighter Easter beam
on our longing eyes shall stream.

Cecil Frances Alexander (1818-1895)

That Easter day 193

1 That Easter day with joy was bright,
the sun shone out with fairer light,
when, to their longing eyes restored,
the apostles saw their risen Lord.

2 His risen flesh with radiance glowed;
his wounded hands and feet he showed;
those scars their solemn witness gave
that Christ was risen from the grave.

3 O Jesus, King of gentleness,
do thou thyself our hearts possess
that we may give thee all our days
the willing tribute of our praise.

4 O Lord of all, with us abide
in this our joyful Eastertide;
from every weapon death can wield
thine own redeemed for ever shield.

5 All praise, O risen Lord, we give
to thee, who, dead, again dost live;
to God the Father equal praise,
and God the Holy Ghost, we raise.

Latin, 5th cent.; Hymnal version, 1939

Come, ye faithful, raise the strain 199

1 Come, ye faithful, raise the strain
of triumphant gladness!
God hath brought his Israel
into joy from sadness:
loosed from Pharaoh's bitter yoke
Jacob's sons and daughters,
led them with unmoistened foot
through the Red Sea waters.

2 'Tis the spring of souls today:
   Christ hath burst his prison,
and from three days' sleep in death
   as a sun hath risen;
all the winter of our sins,
   long and dark, is flying
from his light, to whom we give
   laud and praise undying.

3 Now the queen of seasons, bright
   with the day of splendor,
with the royal feast of feasts,
   comes its joy to render;
comes to glad Jerusalem,
   who with true affection
welcomes in unwearied strains
   Jesus' resurrection.

4 Neither might the gates of death,
   nor the tomb's dark portal,
nor the watchers, nor the seal
   hold thee as a mortal
but today amidst thine own
   thou didst stand, bestowing
that thy peace which evermore
   passeth human knowing.

St. John of Damascus (8th cent.);
tr. John Mason Neale (1818-1866), alt.

Jesus Christ is risen today 207

1 Jesus Christ is risen today, Alleluia!
our triumphant holy day, Alleluia!
who did once upon the cross, Alleluia!
suffer to redeem our loss. Alleluia!

2 Hymns of praise then let us sing, Alleluia!
unto Christ, our heavenly King, Alleluia!
who endured the cross and grave, Alleluia!
sinners to redeem and save. Alleluia!

3 But the pains which he endured, Alleluia!
our salvation have procured, Alleluia!
now above the sky he's King, Alleluia!
where the angels ever sing. Alleluia!

4 Sing we to our God above, Alleluia!
praise eternal as his love, Alleluia!
praise him, all ye heavenly host, Alleluia!
Father, Son, and Holy ghost. Alleluia!

Latin, 14th cent.; tr. Tate and Brady, 1698;
St. 4, Charles Wesley (1707-1788)

The strife is o'er 208

Alleluia, alleluia, alleluia!

1 The strife is o'er, the battle done,
the victory of life is won;
the song of triumph has begun.
Alleluia!

2 The powers of death
have done their worst,
but Christ their legions hath dispersed:
let shout of holy joy outburst.
Alleluia!

3 The three sad days are quickly sped,
he rises glorious from the dead:
all glory to our risen Head!
Alleluia!

4 He closed the yawning gates of hell,
the bars from heaven's high portals fell;
let hymns of praise his triumphs tell!
Alleluia!

5 Lord! by the stripes which wounded thee,
from death's dread sting thy servants free,
that we may live and sing to thee.
Alleluia!

Alleluia, alleluia, alleluia!

Latin, 1695; tr. Francis Pott (1832-1909), alt.

The day of resurrection! 210

1 The day of resurrection!
Earth, tell it out abroad;
the Passover of gladness,
the Passover of God.
From death to life eternal,
from earth unto the sky,
our Christ hath brought us over
with hymns of victory.

2 Our hearts be pure from evil,
that we may see aright
the Lord in rays eternal
of resurrection light;
and, listening to his accents,
may hear so calm and plain
his own "All hail!" and, hearing,
may raise the victor strain.

3 Now let the heavens be joyful,
let earth her song begin,
the round world keep high triumph,
and all that is therein;
let all things seen and unseen
their notes together blend,
for Christ the Lord is risen,
our joy that hath no end.

St. John of Damascus (8th cent.);
tr. John Mason Neale (1818-1866)

Hail thee, festival day! 225

Refrain: Hail thee, festival day!
blest day that art hallowed for ever,
day when the Holy Ghost
shone in the world with God's grace.

1 Lo, in the likeness of fire, on those who
await his appearing,
he whom the Lord foretold
suddenly, swiftly, descends:

Refrain

2 Forth from the Father he comes
with sevenfold mystical offering,
pouring on all human souls
infinite riches of God:

Refrain: Hail thee, festival day!
blest day that art hallowed for ever,
day when the Holy Ghost
shone in the world with God's grace.

3 Hark! for in myriad tongues Christ's own,
his chosen apostles,
preach to the ends of the earth
Christ and his wonderful works:

Refrain

4 Praise to the Spirit of Life, all praise to the
fount of our being,
light that dost lighten all, life that in all
dost abide:

Refrain

Venantius Honorius Fortunatus (540?-600?)

For all the saints 287

1 For all the saints,
who from their labors rest,
who thee by faith
before the world confessed,
thy Name, O Jesus, be for ever blessed.
Alleluia, alleluia!

2 Thou wast their rock,
their fortress, and their might:
thou, Lord, their Captain
in the well-fought fight;
thou, in the darkness drear,
the one true Light.
Alleluia, alleluia!

3 O may thy soldiers, faithful, true, and bold,
fight as the saints who nobly fought of old,
and win, with them,
the victor's crown of gold.
Alleluia, alleluia!

4 O blest communion, fellowship divine!
We feebly struggle, they in glory shine;
yet all are one in thee, for all are thine.
Alleluia, alleluia!

*5 And when the strife is fierce,
the warfare long,
steals on the ear the distant triumph song,
and hearts are brave again,
and arms are strong.
Alleluia, alleluia!

*6 The golden evening brightens in the west;
soon, soon to faithful warriors cometh rest;
sweet is the calm of paradise the blest.
Alleluia, alleluia!

*7 But lo! there breaks
a yet more glorious day;
the saints triumphant rise in bright array;
the King of glory passes on his way.
Alleluia, alleluia!

*8 From earth's wide bounds,
from ocean's farthest coast,
through gates of pearl
streams in the countless host
singing to Father, Son, and Holy Ghost,
Alleluia, alleluia!

William Walsham How (1823-1897)

Come, ye thankful people, come 290

1 Come, ye thankful people, come,
raise the song of harvest-home:
all is safely gathered in,
ere the winter storms begin;
God, our Maker, doth provide
for our wants to be supplied;
come to God's own temple, come,
raise the song of harvest-home.

2 All the world is God's own field,
fruit unto his praise to yield;
wheat and tares together sown,
unto joy or sorrow grown:
first the blade, and then the ear,
then the full corn shall appear:
grant, O harvest Lord, that we
wholesome grain and pure may be.

3 For the Lord our God shall come,
and shall take his harvest home;
from his field shall in that day
all offenses purge away;
give his angels charge at last
in the fire the tares to cast,
but the fruitful ears to store
in his garner evermore.

4 Even so, Lord, quickly come
to thy final harvest-home;
gather thou thy people in,
free from sorrow, free from sin;
there, for ever purified,
in thy presence to abide;
come, with all thine angels, come,
raise the glorious harvest-home.

Henry Alford (1810-1871), alt.

Bread of the world 301

1 Bread of the world, in mercy broken,
Wine of the soul, in mercy shed,
by whom the words of life were spoken,
and in whose death our sins are dead:
look on the heart by sorrow broken,
look on the tears by sinners shed;
and be thy feast to us the token
that by thy grace our souls are fed.

Reginald Heber (1783-1826)

I come with joy to meet my Lord 304

1 I come with joy to meet my Lord,
forgiven, loved, and free,
in awe and wonder to recall
his life laid down for me.

2 I come with Christians far and near
to find, as all are fed,
the new community of love
in Christ's communion bread.

3 As Christ breaks bread and bids us share,
each proud division ends.
That love that made us makes us one,
and strangers now are friends.

4 And thus with joy we meet our Lord.
His presence, always near,
is in such friendship better known:
we see, and praise him here.

5 Together met, together bound,
we'll go our different ways,
and as his people in the world,
we'll live and speak his praise.

Brian A. Wren (b. 1936), alt.

Let us break bread together 325

1 Let us break bread together on our knees;
Let us break bread together on our knees;

when I fall on my knees,
with my face to the rising sun,
O Lord, have mercy on me.

2 Let us drink wine together on our knees;
Let us drink wine together on our knees;

Refrain

3 Let us praise God together on our knees;
Let us praise God together on our knees;

Refrain

Afro-American spiritual

I am the bread of life 335

1 I am the bread of life;
they who come to me shall not hunger;
they who believe in me shall not thirst.
No one can come to me
unless the Father draw them.

And I will raise them up,
and I will raise them up on the
last day.

2 The Bread that I will give
is my Flesh for the life of the world,
and they who eat of this bread,
they shall live for ever.

Refrain

3 Unless you eat
of the Flesh of the Son of Man
and drink of his Blood,
you shall not have life within you.

Refrain

4 I am the resurrection,
I am the life.
They who believe in me,
even if they die,
they shall live for ever.

Refrain

5 Yes, Lord, we believe
that you are the Christ,
the Son of God
who has come into the world.

Refrain

Suzanne Toolan, adapt. from John 6

Holy, holy, holy! 362

1 Holy, holy, holy! Lord God Almighty!
Early in the morning
our song shall rise to thee:
Holy, holy, holy! Merciful and mighty,
God in three Persons, blessed Trinity.

*2 Holy, holy, holy! All the saints adore thee,
casting down their golden crowns
around the glassy sea;
cherubim and seraphim
falling down before thee,
which wert, and art,
and evermore shalt be.

3 Holy, holy, holy!
Though the darkness hide thee,
though the sinful human eye
thy glory may not see,
only thou art holy;
there is none beside thee,
perfect in power, in love, and purity.

4 Holy, holy, holy! Lord God Almighty!
All thy works shall praise thy Name,
in earth, and sky, and sea;
Holy, holy, holy! Merciful and mighty,
God in three Persons, blessed Trinity.

Reginald Heber (1783-1826)

Come, thou almighty King 365

1 Come, thou almighty King,
help us thy Name to sing,
help us to praise.
Father whose love unknown
all things created own,
build in our hearts thy throne,
Ancient of Days.

2 Come, thou incarnate Word,
by heaven and earth adored;
our prayer attend:
come, and thy people bless;
come, give thy word success;
stablish thy righteousness,
Savior and friend.

3 Come, holy Comforter,
thy sacred witness bear
   in this glad hour:
thou, who almighty art,
now rule in every heart,
and ne'er from us depart,
   Spirit of power.

4 To Thee, great One in Three,
the highest praises be,
   hence evermore;
thy sovereign majesty
may we in glory see,
and to eternity
   love and adore.

Anonymous, ca. 1757, alt.

Joyful, joyful, we adore thee 376

1 Joyful, joyful, we adore thee,
God of glory, Lord of love;
hearts unfold like flowers before thee,
praising thee, their sun above.
Melt the clouds of sin and sadness;
drive the dark of doubt away;
giver of immortal gladness,
fill us with the light of day.

2 All thy works with joy surround thee,
earth and heaven reflect thy rays,
Stars and angels sing around thee,
center of unbroken praise.
Field and forest, vale and mountain,
blooming meadow, flashing sea,
chanting bird and flowing fountain,
call us to rejoice in thee.

3 Thou art giving and forgiving,
ever blessing, ever blest,
well-spring of the joy of living,
ocean-depth of happy rest!
Thou our Father, Christ our Brother:
all who live in love are thine;
teach us how to love each other,
lift us to the joy divine.

Henry Van Dyke (1852-1933)

All people that on earth do dwell 377

1 All people that on earth do dwell,
sing to the Lord with cheerful voice:
him serve with mirth, his praise forth tell,
come ye before him and rejoice.

2 Know that the Lord is God indeed;
without our aid he did us make:
we are his folk, he doth us feed,
and for his sheep he doth us take.

3 O enter then his gates with praise,
approach with joy his courts unto;
praise, laud, and bless his Name always,
for it is seemly so to do.

4 For why? the Lord our God is good,
his mercy is for ever sure;
his truth at all times firmly stood,
and shall from age to age endure.

*5 To Father, Son, and Holy Ghost,
the God whom heaven
and earth adore,
from men and from the angel host
be praise and glory evermore.

William Kethe (d. 1608?); based on Psalm 100

Fairest Lord Jesus 383

1 Fairest Lord Jesus,
Ruler of all nature,
O thou of God and man the Son;
thee will I cherish,
thee will I honor,
thou, my soul's glory, joy, and crown.

2 Fair are the meadows,
fairer still the woodlands,
robed in the blooming garb of spring:
Jesus is fairer,
Jesus is purer,
who makes the woeful heart to sing.

3 Fair is the sunshine,
fairer still the moonlight,
and all the twinkling, starry host:
Jesus shines brighter,
Jesus shines purer,
than all the angels heaven can boast.

St. 1, Munster, 1677;
Sts. 2 & 3, Leipzig, 1842; Tr. pub. New York, 1850, alt.

O worship the King 388

1 O worship the King, all glorious above!
O gratefully sing his power and his love!
Our shield and defender,
the Ancient of Days,
pavilioned in splendor,
and girded with praise.

2 O tell of his might! O sing of his grace!
Whose robe is the light,
whose canopy space.
His chariots of wrath
the deep thunderclouds form,
and dark is his path
on the wings of the storm.

3 The earth, with its store of wonders untold,
Almighty, thy power hath founded of old,
hath stablished it fast
by a changeless decree,
and round it hath cast,
like a mantle, the sea.

4 Thy bountiful care,
what tongue can recite?
It breathes in the air; it shines in the light;
it streams from the hills,
it descends to the plain,
and sweetly distills in the dew and the rain.

4 Frail children of dust, and feeble as frail,
in thee do we trust, nor find thee to fail;
thy mercies, how tender!
how firm to the end!
Our Maker, Defender,
Redeemer, and Friend!

Robert Grant (1779-1838); based on Psalm 104

Praise to the Lord 390

1 Praise to the Lord, the Almighty,
the King of creation;
O my soul, praise him,
for he is thy health and salvation:
join the great throng,
psaltery, organ, and song,
sounding in glad adoration.

2 Praise to the Lord;
over all things he gloriously reigneth:
borne as on eagle-wings,
safely his saints he sustaineth.
Hast thou not seen
how all thou needest hath been
granted in what he ordaineth?

3 Praise to the Lord,
who doth prosper thy way
and defend thee;
surely his goodness and mercy
shall ever attend thee;
ponder anew
what the Almighty can do,
who with his love doth befriend thee.

4 Praise to the Lord!
O let all that is in me adore him!
All that hath life and breath
come now with praises before him!
Let the amen
sound from his people again;
gladly for ever adore him.

Joachim Neander (1650-1680);
Hymnal version, 1939, alt.;
based on Psalms 103 and 150

Now thank we all our God 397

1 Now thank we all our God,
with heart, and hands, and voices,
who wondrous things hath done,
in whom his world rejoices;
who from our mother's arms
hath blessed us on our way
with countless gifts of love,
and still is ours today.

2 O may this bounteous God
through all our life be near us!
With ever-joyful hearts
and blessed peace to cheer us;
and keep us in his grace,
and guide us when perplexed,
and free us from all ills
in this world and the next.

3 All praise and thanks to God
the Father now be given,
the Son, and him who reigns
with them in highest heaven,
eternal, Triune God,
whom earth and heaven adore;
for thus it was, is now,
and shall be, evermore.

Martin Rinkart (1586-1649);
tr. Catherine Winkworth (1827-1878)

The God of Abraham praise 401

1 The God of Abraham praise,
who reigns enthroned above;
Ancient of everlasting days,
and God of love;
the Lord, the great I AM,
by earth and heaven confessed:
we bow and bless the sacred Name
for ever blest.

2 He by himself hath sworn:
we on his oath depend;
we shall, on eagle-wings upborne,
to heaven ascend:
we shall behold his face,
we shall his power adore,
and sing the wonders of his grace
for evermore.

3 There dwells the Lord, our King,
the Lord, our Righteousness,
triumphant o'er the world and sin,
the Prince of Peace;
on Zion's sacred height
his kingdom he maintains,
and, glorious with his saints in light,
for ever reigns.

4 The God who reigns on high
the great archangels sing,
and "Holy, holy, holy," cry,
"Almighty King!
Who was, and is, the same,
and evermore shall be:
eternal Father, great I AM,
we worship thee."

5 The whole triumphant host
give thanks to God on high;
"Hail, Father, Son, and Holy Ghost!"
they ever cry;
hail, Abraham's Lord divine!
With heaven our songs we raise;
all might and majesty are thine,
and endless praise.

Thomas Olivers (1725-1799), alt.

All things bright and beautiful 405

Refrain: All things bright and beautiful,
all creatures great and small,
all things wise and wonderful,
the Lord God made them all.

1 Each little flower that opens,
each little bird that sings,
he made their glowing colors,
he made their tiny wings.

Refrain

2 The purple-headed mountain,
the river running by,
the sunset, and the morning
that brightens up the sky,

Refrain: All things bright and beautiful,
all creatures great and small,
all things wise and wonderful,
the Lord God made them all.

3 The cold wind in the winter,
the pleasant summer sun,
the ripe fruits in the garden,
he made them every one.

Refrain

4 He gave us eyes to see them,
and lips that we might tell
how great is God Almighty,
who has made all things well.

Refrain

Cecil Frances Alexander (1818-1895)

Praise, my soul, the King of heaven 410

1 Praise, my soul, the King of heaven;
to his feet thy tribute bring;
ransomed, healed, restored, forgiven,
evermore his praises sing:
Alleluia, alleluia!
Praise the everlasting King.

2 Praise him for his grace and favor
to his people in distress;
praise him still, the same as ever,
slow to chide, and swift to bless:
Alleluia, alleluia!
Glorious in his faithfulness.

3 Father-like he tends and spares us;
well our feeble frame he knows;
in his hand he gently bears us,
rescues us from all our foes.
Alleluia, alleluia!
Widely yet his mercy flows.

4 Angels, help us to adore him;
ye behold him face to face;
sun and moon, bow down before him,
dwellers all in time and space.
Alleluia, alleluia!
Praise with us the God of grace.

Henry Francis Lyte (1793-1847), alt.;
based on Psalm 103

When morning gilds the skies 427

1 When morning gilds the skies,
my heart, awaking, cries,
may Jesus Christ be praised!
When evening shadows fall,
this rings my curfew call,
may Jesus Christ be praised!

2 When mirth for music longs,
this is my song of songs:
may Jesus Christ be praised!
God's holy house of prayer
hath none that can compare
with: Jesus Christ be praised!

3 No lovelier antiphon
in all high heaven is known
  than, Jesus Christ be praised!
There to the eternal Word
the eternal psalm is heard:
  may Jesus Christ be praised!

4 Ye nations of mankind,
in this your concord find:
  may Jesus Christ be praised!
Let all the earth around
ring joyous with the sound:
  may Jesus Christ be praised!

4 Sing, suns and stars of space,
sing, ye that see his face,
  sing, Jesus Christ be praised!
God's whole creation o'er,
both now and evermore
  shall Jesus Christ be praised!

German, ca. 1800; tr. Robert Seymour Bridges (1844-1930), alt.

We gather together

1 We gather together
to ask the Lord's blessing;
he chastens and hastens
his will to make known;
the wicked oppressing
now cease from distressing:
sing praises to his Name;
he forgets not his own.

2 Beside us to guide us,
our God with us joining,
ordaining, maintaining
his kingdom divine;
so from the beginning
the fight we were winning:
thou, Lord, wast at our side:
all glory be thine!

3 We all do extol thee,
thou leader triumphant,
and pray that thou still
our defender wilt be.
Let thy congregation escape tribulation:
thy Name be ever praised!
O Lord, make us free!

Anonymous, 1625; tr. Theodore Baker (1851-1934)

Alleluia! sing to Jesus! 460

1 Alleluia! sing to Jesus!
his the scepter, his the throne;
Alleluia! his the triumph,
his the victory alone;
Hark! the songs of peaceful Zion
thunder like a mighty flood;
Jesus out of every nation
hath redeemed us by his blood.

*2 Alleluia! not as orphans
are we left in sorrow now;
Alleluia! he is near us,
faith believes, nor questions how:
though the cloud from sight received him,
when the forty days were o'er,
shall our hearts forget his promise,
"I am with you evermore"?

3 Alleluia! Bread of Heaven,
Thou on earth our food, our stay!
Alleluia! here the sinful
flee to thee from day to day:
Intercessor, friend of sinners,
earth's Redeemer, plead for me,
where the songs of all the sinless
sweep across the crystal sea.

4 Alleluia! King eternal,
thee the Lord of lords we own:
Alleluia! born of Mary,
earth thy footstool, heaven thy throne:
thou within the veil hast entered,
robed in flesh, our great High Priest:
thou on earth both Priest and Victim
in the eucharistic feast.

*5 Alleluia! sing to Jesus!
his the scepter, his the throne;
Alleluia! his the triumph,
his the victory alone;
Hark! the songs of holy Zion
thunder like a mighty flood;
Jesus out of every nation
hath redeemed us by his blood.

William Chatterton Dix (1837-1898)

There's a wideness in God's mercy 470

1 There's a wideness in God's mercy
like the wideness of the sea;
there's a kindness in his justice,
which is more than liberty.
There is welcome for the sinner,
and more graces for the good;
there is mercy with the Savior;
there is healing in his blood.

2 There is no place where earth's sorrows
are more felt than up in heaven;
there is no place where earth's failings
have such kindly judgment given.
There is plentiful redemption
in the blood that has been shed;
there is joy for all the members
in the sorrows of the Head.

3 For the love of God is broader
than the measure of the mind;
and the heart of the Eternal
is most wonderfully kind.
If our love were but more faithful,
we should take him at his word;
and our life would be thanksgiving
for the goodness of the Lord.

Frederick William Faber (1814-1863), alt.

Lift high the cross 473

Refrain: Lift high the cross,
the love of Christ proclaim
till all the world adore
his sacred Name.

1 Led on their way by this triumphant sign,
the hosts of God
in conquering ranks combine.

Refrain

2 Each new-born servant of the Crucified
bears on the brow
the seal of him who died.

Refrain: Lift high the cross,
the love of Christ proclaim
till all the world adore
his sacred Name.

3 O Lord, once lifted on the glorious tree,
as thou hast promised,
draw the world to thee.

Refrain

4 So shall our song of triumph ever be:
praise to the Crucified for victory.

Refrain

George William Kitchin (1827-1912)
and Michael Robert Newbolt (1874-1956), alt.

When I survey the wondrous cross 474

1 When I survey the wondrous cross
where the young Prince of Glory died,
my richest gain I count but loss,
and pour contempt on all my pride.

2 Forbid it, Lord, that I should boast,
save in the cross of Christ, my God:
all the vain things that charm me most,
I sacrifice them to his blood.

3 See, from his head, his hands, his feet
sorrow and love flow mingled down!
Did e'er such love and sorrow meet,
or thorns compose so rich a crown?

4 Were the whole realm of nature mine,
that were an offering far too small;
love so amazing, so divine,
demands my soul, my life, my all.

Isaac Watts (1674-1748)

Lord of all hopefulness 482

1 Lord of all hopefulness, Lord of all joy,
whose trust, ever child-like,
no cares could destroy,
be there at our waking,
and give us, we pray,
your bliss in our hearts, Lord, at the break
of the day.

2 Lord of all eagerness, Lord of all faith,
whose strong hands were skilled
at the plane and the lathe,
be there at our labors,
and give us, we pray,
your strength in our hearts,
Lord, at the noon of the day.

3 Lord of all kindliness, Lord of all grace,
your hands swift to welcome, your arms to
embrace,
be there at our homing,
and give us, we pray,
your love in our hearts, Lord, at the eve
of the day.

4 Lord of all gentleness, Lord of all calm,
whose voice is contentment,
whose presence is balm,
be there at our sleeping,
and give us, we pray,
your peace in our hearts, Lord,
at the end of the day.

Jan Struther (1901-1953)

O for a thousand tongues to sing 493

1 O for a thousand tongues to sing
my dear Redeemer's praise,
the glories of my God and King,
the triumphs of his grace!

2 My gracious Master and my God,
assist me to proclaim
and spread through all the earth
abroad the honors of thy Name.

3 Jesus! the Name that charms our fears
and bids our sorrows cease;
'tis music in the sinner's ears,
'tis life and health and peace.

4 He speaks; and, listening to his voice,
new life the dead receive,
the mournful broken hearts rejoice,
the humble poor believe.

5 Hear him, ye deaf; ye voiceless ones,
your loosened tongues employ;
ye blind, behold, your Savior comes;
and leap, ye lame, for joy!

6 Glory to God and praise and love
be now and ever given
by saints below and saints above,
the Church in earth and heaven.

Charles Wesley (1707-1788), alt.

Crown him with many crowns 494

1 Crown him with many crowns,
the Lamb upon his throne;
Hark! how the heavenly anthem drowns
all music but its own;
awake, my soul, and sing
of him who died for thee,
and hail him as thy matchless King
through all eternity.

2 Crown him the Son of God
before the worlds began,
and ye, who tread where he hath trod,
crown him the Son of man;
who every grief hath known
that wrings the human breast,
and takes and bears them for his own,
that all in him may rest.

3 Crown him the Lord of life,
who triumphed o'er the grave,
and rose victorious in the strife
for those he came to save;
his glories now we sing
who died, and rose on high,
who died, eternal life to bring,
and lives that death may die.

4 Crown him of lords the Lord,
who over all doth reign,
who once on earth, the incarnate Word,
for ransomed sinners slain,
now lives in realms of light,
where saints with angels sing
their songs before him day and night,
their God, Redeemer, King.

5 Crown him the Lord of heaven,
enthroned in worlds above;
Crown him the King, to whom is given
the wondrous name of Love.
Crown him with many crowns,
as thrones before him fall,
crown him, ye kings, with many crowns,
for he is King of all.

Matthew Bridges (1800-1894)

Beneath the cross of Jesus 498

1 Beneath the cross of Jesus
I fain would take my stand,
the shadow of a mighty rock
within a weary land,
a home within the wilderness,
a rest upon the way,
from the burning of the noontide heat,
and the burden of the day.

2 Upon the cross of Jesus
   mine eyes at times can see
the very dying form of one
   who suffered there for me;
and from my smitten heart with tears
   two wonders I confess:
the wonders of redeeming love,
   and my unworthiness.

3 I take, O cross, thy shadow
   for my abiding place;
I ask no other sunshine than
   the sunshine of his face;
content to let my pride go by,
   to know no gain nor loss,
my sinful self my only shame,
   my glory all the cross.

Elizabeth Cecilia Clephane (1830-1869), alt.

Glorious things of thee are spoken 522

1 Glorious things of thee are spoken,
Zion, city of our God;
he whose word cannot be broken
formed thee for his own abode;
on the Rock of Ages founded,
what can shake thy sure repose?
With salvation's walls surrounded,
thou may'st smile at all thy foes.

2 See! the streams of living waters,
springing from eternal love,
well supply thy sons and daughters
and all fear of want remove.
Who can faint, when such a river
ever will their thirst assuage?
Grace which, like the Lord, the giver
never fails from age to age.

3 Round each habitation hovering,
see the cloud and fire appear
for a glory and a covering,
showing that the Lord is near.
Thus deriving from their banner,
light by night, and shade by day,
safe they feed upon the manna
which he gives them when they pray.

4 Blest inhabitants of Zion,
washed in the Redeemer's blood!
Jesus, whom their souls rely on,
makes them kings and priests to God.
'Tis his love his people raises
over self to reign as kings:
and as priests, his solemn praises
each for a thank-offering brings.

John Newton (1725-1807)

I love thy kingdom, Lord 524

1 I love thy kingdom, Lord,
the house of thine abode,
the Church our blest Redeemer saved
with his own precious blood.

2 For her my tears shall fall;
for her my prayers ascend;
to her my cares and toils be given,
till toils and cares shall end.

3 Beyond my highest joy
I prize her heavenly ways,
her sweet communion, solemn vows,
her hymns of love and praise.

4 Jesus, thou friend divine,
our Savior and our King,
thy hand from every snare and foe
shall great deliverance bring.

5 Sure as thy truth shall last,
to Zion shall be given
the brightest glories earth can yield,
and brighter bliss of heaven.

Timothy Dwight (1725-1817);
based on Psalm 137

In Christ there is no East or West 529

1 In Christ there is no East or West,
in him no South or North,
but one great fellowship of love
throughout the whole wide earth.

2 Join hands, disciples of the faith,
whate'er your race may be!
Who serves my Father as his child
is surely kin to me.

3 In Christ now meet both East and West,
in him meet South and North,
all Christly souls are one in him,
throughout the whole wide earth.

John Oxenham (1852-1941), alt.

O Spirit of the living God 531

1 O Spirit of the living God,
in all thy plenitude of grace,
where'er the foot of man hath trod,
descend on our apostate race.

2 Give tongues of fire and hearts of love,
to preach the reconciling word;
give power and unction from above,
whene'er the joyful sound is heard.

3 Be darkness, at thy coming, light;
confusion, order in thy path;
souls without strength inspire with might,
bid mercy triumph over wrath.

4 Convert the nations! far and nigh
the triumphs of the cross record;
the Name of Jesus glorify,
till every people call him Lord.

James Montgomery (1771-1854), alt.

How wondrous and great thy works 533

1 How wondrous and great thy works,
God of praise!
How just, King of saints,
and true are thy ways!
O who shall not fear thee,
and honor thy Name?
Thou only art holy, thou only supreme.

2 To nations of earth
thy light shall be shown;
their worship and vows
shall come to thy throne:
thy truth and thy judgments
shall spread all abroad,
till earth's every people
confess thee their God.

Henry Ustick Onderdonk (1759-1858), alt.

Christ for the world we sing! 537

1 Christ for the world we sing!
The world to Christ we bring
with loving zeal;
the poor, and them that mourn,
the faint and overborne,
sin-sick and sorrow-worn,
whom Christ doth heal.

2 Christ for the world we sing!
The world to Christ we bring
with fervent prayer;
the wayward and the lost,
by restless passions tossed,
redeemed at countless cost
from dark despair.

3 Christ for the world we sing!
The world to Christ we bring
with one accord;
with us the work to share,
with us reproach to dare,
with us the cross to bear,
for Christ the Lord.

4 Christ for the world we sing!
The world to Christ we bring
with joyful song;
the new-born souls, whose days,
reclaimed from error's ways,
inspired with hope and praise,
to Christ belong.

Samuel Wolcott (1813-1886)

Jesus shall reign 544

1 Jesus shall reign where'er the sun
doth his successive journeys run;
his kingdom stretch from shore to shore,
till moons shall wax and wane no more.

2 To him shall endless prayer be made,
and praises throng to crown his head;
his Name like sweet perfume shall rise
with every morning sacrifice.

3 People and realms of every tongue
dwell on his love with sweetest song;
and infant voices shall proclaim
their early blessings on his Name.

4 Blessings abound where'er he reigns:
the prisoners leap to lose their chains,
the weary find eternal rest,
and all who suffer want are blest.

5 Let every creature rise and bring
peculiar honors to our King;
angels descend with songs again,
and earth repeat the loud amen.

Isaac Watts (1674-1748), alt.

Awake, my soul 546

1 Awake, my soul, stretch every nerve,
and press with vigor on;
a heavenly race demands thy zeal,
and an immortal crown.

2 A cloud of witnesses around
hold thee in full survey;
forget the steps already trod
and onward urge thy way.

3 'Tis God's all-animating voice
that calls thee from on high;
'Tis his own hand presents the prize
to thine aspiring eye.

4 Then wake, my soul, stretch every nerve,
and press with vigor on;
a heavenly race demands thy zeal,
and an immortal crown.

Philip Doddridge (1702-1751)

Fight the good fight 553

1 Fight the good fight with all thy might,
Christ is thy strength and Christ thy right;
lay hold on life, and it shall be
thy joy and crown eternally.

2 Run the straight race
through God's good grace,
lift up thine eyes and seek his face;
life with its way before us lies,
Christ is the path and Christ the prize.

*3 Cast care aside, lean on thy Guide;
his boundless mercy will provide;
trust, and thy trusting soul shall prove
Christ is its life and Christ its love.

*4 Faint not nor fear, his arms are near;
he changeth not, and thou art dear;
only believe, and thou shalt see
that Christ is all in all to thee.

John Samuel Bewley Monsell (1811-1875)

Lead on, O King eternal 555

1 Lead on, O King eternal,
 the day of march has come;
henceforth in fields of conquest
 thy tents shall be our home:
through days of preparation
 thy grace has made us strong,
and now, O King eternal,
 we lift our battle-song.

2 Lead on, O King eternal,
till sin's fierce war shall cease,
and holiness shall whisper
the sweet amen of peace;
for not with swords loud clashing,
nor roll of stirring drums,
but deeds of love and mercy,
the heavenly kingdom comes.

3 Lead on, O King eternal:
we follow, not with fears;
for gladness breaks like morning
where'er thy face appears.
Thy cross is lifted o'er us;
we journey in its light:
the crown awaits the conquest;
lead on, O God of might!

Ernest Warburton Shurtleff (1862-1917)

Rejoice, ye pure in heart! 556

1 Rejoice, ye pure in heart!
Rejoice, give thanks, and sing!
Your glorious banner wave on high,
the cross of Christ your King.

Rejoice, rejoice,
rejoice, give thanks, and sing.

2 With all the angel choirs,
with all the saints of earth,
pour out the strains of joy and bliss,
true rapture, noblest mirth.

Refrain

3 Your clear hosannas raise,
and alleluias loud;
while answering echoes upward float,
like wreaths of incense cloud.

Refrain

4 Yes, on through life's long path,
still chanting as ye go,
from youth to age, by night and day,
in gladness and in woe.

Refrain

5 Still lift your standard high,
still march in firm array,
as warriors through the darkness toil,
till dawns the golden day.

Refrain

*6 At last the march shall end;
the wearied ones shall rest;
the pilgrims find their Father's house,
Jerusalem the blest.

Refrain

*7 Then on, ye pure in heart!
Rejoice, give thanks, and sing!
Your glorious banner wave on high
the cross of Christ your King.

Refrain

Edward Hayes Plumptre (1821-1891)

Faith of our fathers! 558

1 Faith of our fathers! living still
in spite of dungeon, fire and sword:
O how our hearts beat high with joy,
whene'er we hear that glorious word:

Faith of our fathers, holy faith!
We will be true to thee till death.

2 Faith of our fathers! faith and prayer
shall win all nations unto thee;
and through the truth
that comes from God,
mankind shall then indeed be free.

Refrain

3 Faith of our fathers! we will love
both friend and foe in all our strife:
and preach thee, too, as love knows how,
by kindly deeds and virtuous life.

Refrain

Frederick William Faber (1814-1863)

Lead us, heavenly Father, lead us 559

1 Lead us, heavenly Father, lead us
o'er the world's tempestuous sea;
guard us, guide us, keep us, feed us,
for we have no help but thee,
yet possessing every blessing,
if our God our Father be.

2 Savior, breathe forgiveness o'er us;
all our weakness thou dost know;
thou didst tread this earth before us;
thou didst feel its keenest woe;
yet unfearing, persevering,
to thy passion thou didst go.

3 Spirit of our God, descending,
fill our hearts with heavenly joy;
love with every passion bending,
pleasure that can never cloy;
thus provided, pardoned, guided,
nothing can our peace destroy.

James Edmeston (1791-1867), alt.

Onward, Christian soldiers 562

1 Onward, Christian soldiers,
marching as to war,
with the cross of Jesus
going on before!
Christ, the royal Master,
leads against the foe;
forward into battle,
see, his banners go.

Onward, Christian soldiers,
marching as to war,
with the cross of Jesus
going on before!

*2 At the sign of triumph
Satan's host doth flee;
on, then, Christian soldiers,
on to victory!
Hell's foundations quiver
at the shout of praise;
Christians, lift your voices,
loud your anthems raise.

Refrain

*3 Like a mighty army
moves the Church of God;
Christians, we are treading
where the saints have trod;
we are not divided,
all one body we,
one in hope and doctrine,
one in charity.

Refrain

4 Crowns and thrones may perish,
kingdoms rise and wane,
but the Church of Jesus
constant will remain;
gates of hell can never
'gainst that Church prevail;
we have Christ's own promise,
and that cannot fail.

Refrain

5 Onward, then, ye people,
join our happy throng;
blend with ours your voices
in the triumph song:
glory, laud, and honor,
unto Christ the King;
this through countless ages
we with angels sing.

Onward, Christian soldiers,
marching as to war,
with the cross of Jesus
going on before!

Sabine Baring-Gould (1834-1924), alt.

He who would valiant be 564

1 He who would valiant be
'gainst all disaster,
let him in constancy
follow the Master.
There's no discouragement
shall make him once relent
his first avowed intent
to be a pilgrim.

2 Who so beset him round
with dismal stories,
do but themselves confound,
his strength the more is.
No foes shall stay his might,
though he with giants fight;
he will make good his right
to be a pilgrim.

3 Since, Lord, thou dost defend
us with thy Spirit,
we know we at the end
shall life inherit.
Then fancies flee away;
I'll fear not what men say,
I'll labor night and day
to be a pilgrim.

Percy Dearmer (1867-1936),
after John Bunyan (1628-1688)

God of grace and God of glory 594

1 God of grace and God of glory,
on thy people pour thy power;
crown thine ancient Church's story;
bring her bud to glorious flower.
Grant us wisdom, grant us courage,
for the facing of this hour.

2 Lo! the hosts of evil round us
scorn thy Christ, assail his ways!
From the fears that long have bound us
free our hearts to faith and praise:
grant us wisdom, grant us courage
for the living of these days.

3 Cure thy children's warring madness,
bend our pride to thy control;
shame our wanton, selfish gladness,
rich in things and poor in soul.
Grant us wisdom, grant us courage,
lest we miss thy kingdom's goal.

4 Save us from weak resignation
to the evils we deplore;
let the gift of thy salvation
be our glory evermore.
Grant us wisdom, grant us courage,
serving thee whom we adore.

Harry Emerson Fosdick (1878-1969), alt.

Eternal Father, strong to save 608

1 Eternal Father, strong to save,
whose arm hath bound the restless wave,
who bidd'st the mighty ocean deep
its own appointed limits keep:
O hear us when we cry to thee
for those in peril on the sea.

2 O Christ, whose voice the waters heard
and hushed their raging at thy word,
who walkedst on the foaming deep,
and calm amid its rage didst sleep:
O hear us when we cry to thee
for those in peril on the sea.

3 Most Holy Spirit, who didst brood
upon the chaos dark and rude,
and bid its angry tumult cease,
and give, for wild confusion, peace;
O hear us when we cry to thee
for those in peril on the sea.

4 O Trinity of love and power,
thy children shield in danger's hour;
from rock and tempest, fire and foe,
protect them wheresoe'er they go;
thus evermore shall rise to thee
glad hymns of praise
from land and sea.

William Whiting (1825-1878), alt.

Thy kingdom come, O God! 613

1 Thy kingdom come, O God!
Thy rule, O Christ, begin!
Break with thine iron rod
the tyrannies of sin!

2 Where is thy reign of peace,
and purity, and love?
When shall all hatred cease,
as in the realms above?

3 When comes the promised time
that war shall be no more,
oppression, lust, and crime
shall flee thy face before?

4 We pray thee, Lord, arise,
and come in thy great might;
revive our longing eyes,
which languish for thy sight.

5 Wherever near or far
thick darkness broodeth yet:
arise, O Morning Star,
arise, and never set!

Lewis Hensley (1824-1905), alt.

Ye watchers and ye holy ones 618

1 Ye watchers and ye holy ones,
bright seraphs, cherubim, and thrones,
raise the glad strain, Alleluia!
Cry out, dominions, princedoms, powers,
virtues, archangels, angels' choirs,
Alleluia, alleluia, alleluia, alleluia
alleluia!

2 O higher than the cherubim,
more glorious than the seraphim,
lead their praises, Alleluia!
Thou bearer of the eternal Word,
most gracious, magnify the Lord,
Alleluia, alleluia, alleluia, alleluia
alleluia!

3 Respond, ye souls in endless rest,
ye patriarchs and prophets blest,
Alleluia, alleluia!
Ye holy twelve, ye martyrs strong,
all saints triumphant, raise the song,
Alleluia, alleluia, alleluia, alleluia,
alleluia!

4 O friends, in gladness let us sing,
supernal anthems echoing,
Alleluia, alleluia!
To God the Father, God the Son,
and God the Spirit, Three in One,
Alleluia, alleluia, alleluia, alleluia,
alleluia!

John Athelstan Laurie Riley (1858-1945), alt.

How firm a foundation 636

1 How firm a foundation,
ye saints of the Lord,
is laid for your faith in his excellent word!
What more can he say
than to you he hath said,
to you that for refuge to Jesus have fled?

2 "Fear not, I am with thee;
O be not dismayed!
For I am thy God,
and will still give thee aid;
I'll strengthen thee, help thee,
and cause thee to stand,
upheld by my righteous, omnipotent hand.

3 “When through the deep waters
I call thee to go,
the rivers of woe shall not thee overflow;
for I will be with thee, thy troubles to bless,
and sanctify to thee thy deepest distress.

4 “When through fiery trials
thy pathway shall lie,
my grace, all-sufficient, shall be thy supply;
the flame shall not hurt thee; I only design
thy dross to consume,
and thy gold to refine.

5 “The soul that to Jesus
hath fled for repose,
I will not, I will not desert to its foes;
that soul,
though all hell shall endeavor to shake,
I'll never, no, never, no, never forsake.”

K. in John Rippon's *Selection,* 1787, alt.

The King of love my shepherd is 645

1 The King of love my shepherd is,
whose goodness faileth never;
I nothing lack if I am his,
and he is mine for ever.

2 Where streams of living water flow,
my ransomed soul he leadeth,
and where the verdant pastures grow,
with food celestial feedeth.

*3 Perverse and foolish oft I strayed,
but yet in love he sought me,
and on his shoulder gently laid,
and home, rejoicing, brought me.

*4 In death's dark vale I fear no ill
with thee, dear Lord, beside me;
thy rod and staff my comfort still,
thy cross before to guide me.

5 Thou spread'st a table in my sight;
thy unction grace bestoweth;
and oh, what transport of delight
from thy pure chalice floweth!

6 And so through all the length of days
thy goodness faileth never:
Good Shepherd, may I sing thy praise
within thy house for ever.

Henry Williams Baker (1821-1877) based on Psalm 23

Dear Lord and Father of mankind 653

1 Dear Lord and Father of mankind,
forgive our foolish ways!
Reclothe us in our rightful mind,
in purer lives thy service find,
in deeper reverence, praise.

2 In simple trust like theirs who heard,
beside the Syrian sea,
the gracious calling of the Lord,
let us, like them, without a word,
rise up and follow thee.

3 O Sabbath rest by Galilee!
O calm of hills above,
where Jesus knelt to share with thee
the silence of eternity
interpreted by love!

4 Drop thy still dews of quietness,
till all our strivings cease;
take from our souls the strain and stress,
and let our ordered lives confess
the beauty of thy peace.

5 Breathe through the heats of our desire
thy coolness and thy balm;
let sense be dumb, let flesh retire;
speak through the earthquake,
wind, and fire,
O still, small voice of calm.

John Greenleaf Whittier (1807-1892), alt.

Love divine, all loves excelling 657

1 Love divine, all loves excelling,
joy of heaven, to earth come down,
fix in us thy humble dwelling,
all thy faithful mercies crown.
Jesus, thou art all compassion,
pure, unbounded love thou art;
visit us with thy salvation,
enter every trembling heart.

2 Come, almighty to deliver,
let us all thy life receive;
suddenly return, and never,
nevermore thy temples leave.
Thee we would be alway blessing,
serve thee as thy hosts above,
pray, and praise thee without ceasing,
glory in thy perfect love.

3 Finish then thy new creation;
pure and spotless let us be;
let us see thy great salvation
perfectly restored in thee:
changed from glory into glory,
till in heaven we take our place,
till we cast our crowns before thee,
lost in wonder, love, and praise.

Charles Wesley (1707-1788)

O Master, let me walk with thee 660

1 O Master, let me walk with thee
in lowly paths of service free;
tell me thy secret; help me bear
the strain of toil, the fret of care.

2 Help me the slow of heart to move
by some clear, winning word of love;
teach me the wayward feet to stay,
and guide them in the homeward way.

3 Teach me thy patience; still with thee
in closer, dearer company,
in work that keeps faith sweet and strong,
in trust that triumphs over wrong,

4 in hope that sends a shining ray
far down the future's broadening way,
in peace that only thou canst give,
with thee, O Master, let me live.

Washington Gladden (1836-1918)

Abide with me 662

1 Abide with me: fast falls the eventide;
the darkness deepens;
  Lord, with me abide:
when other helpers fail and comforts flee,
help of the helpless, O abide with me.

2 I need thy presence every passing hour;
what but thy grace can
  foil the tempter's power?
Who, like thyself,
  my guide and stay can be?
Through cloud and sunshine, Lord,
  abide with me.

3 I fear no foe, with thee at hand to bless;
ills have no weight,
  and tears no bitterness.
Where is death's sting?
  Where, grave, thy victory?
I triumph still, if thou abide with me.

4 Hold thou thy cross
  before my closing eyes;
shine through the gloom,
  and point me to the skies;
heaven's morning breaks,
  and earth's vain shadows flee;
in life, in death, O Lord, abide with me.

Henry Frances Lyte (1793-1847)

Amazing grace! 671

1 Amazing grace! how sweet the sound,
  that saved a wretch like me!
I once was lost but now am found,
  was blind but now I see.

2 'Twas grace that taught my heart to fear,
and grace my fears relieved;
how precious did that grace appear
the hour I first believed!

3 The Lord has promised good to me,
his word my hope secures;
he will my shield and portion be
as long as life endures.

4 Through many dangers, toils, and snares,
I have already come;
'tis grace that brought me safe thus far,
and grace will lead me home.

*5 When we've been there
ten thousand years,
bright shining as the sun,
we've no less days to sing God's praise
than when we'd first begun.

Sts. 1-4, John Newton (1725-1807), alt.;
St. 5, John Rees (19th cent.)

O God, our help in ages past 680

1 O God, our help in ages past,
our hope for years to come,
our shelter from the stormy blast,
and our eternal home:

2 under the shadow of thy throne
thy saints have dwelt secure;
sufficient is thine arm alone,
and our defense is sure.

3 Before the hills in order stood,
or earth received her frame,
from everlasting thou art God,
to endless years the same.

4 A thousand ages in thy sight
are like an evening gone;
short as the watch that ends the night
before the rising sun.

5 Time, like an ever-rolling stream,
bears all our years away;
they fly, forgotten, as a dream
dies at the opening day.

6 O God, our help in ages past,
our hope for years to come,
be thou our guide while life shall last,
and our eternal home.

Isaac Watts (1674-1748), alt.; based on Psalm 90

Rock of ages 685

1 Rock of ages, cleft for me,
let me hide myself in thee;
let the water and the blood
from thy wounded side that flowed,
be of sin the double cure,
cleanse me from its guilt and power.

2 Should my tears for ever flow,
should my zeal no languor know,
all for sin could not atone:
thou must save, and thou alone;
in my hand no price I bring,
simply to thy cross I cling.

3 While I draw this fleeting breath,
when mine eyelids close in death,
when I rise to worlds unknown
and behold thee on thy throne,
Rock of ages, cleft for me,
let me hide myself in thee.

Augustus Montague Toplady, (1740-1778), alt.

A mighty fortress is our God 688

1 A mighty fortress is our God,
  a bulwark never failing;
our helper he amid the flood
  of mortal ills prevailing:
for still our ancient foe
doth seek to work us woe;
his craft and power are great,
and, armed with cruel hate,
  on earth is not his equal.

2 Did we in our own strength confide,
  our striving would be losing;
were not the right man on our side,
  the man of God's own choosing:
dost ask who that may be?
Christ Jesus, it is he;
Lord Sabaoth his Name,
from age to age the same,
  and he must win the battle.

3 And though this world, with devils filled,
should threaten to undo us;
we will not fear, for God hath willed
his truth to triumph through us;
the prince of darkness grim,
we tremble not for him;
his rage we can endure,
for lo! his doom is sure,
one little word shall fell him.

4 That word above all earthly powers,
no thanks to them, abideth;
the Spirit and the gifts are ours
through him who with us sideth:
let goods and kindred go,
this mortal life also;
the body they may kill:
God's truth abideth still,
his kingdom is for ever.

Martin Luther (1483-1546);
tr. Frederic Henry Hedge (1805-1890);
based on Psalm 46

My faith looks up to thee 691

1 My faith looks up to thee,
thou Lamb of Calvary,
Savior divine!
Now hear me while I pray,
take all my guilt away;
O let me from this day
be wholly thine.

2 May thy rich grace impart
strength to my fainting heart,
my zeal inspire;
as thou hast died for me,
O may my love to thee
pure, warm, and changeless be,
a living fire.

3 While life's dark maze I tread,
and griefs around me spread,
be thou my guide;
bid darkness turn to day;
wipe sorrow's tears away,
nor let me ever stray
from thee aside.

Ray Palmer (1808-1887)

Just as I am 693

1 Just as I am, without one plea,
but that thy blood was shed for me,
and that thou bidd'st me come to thee,
O Lamb of God, I come.

2 Just as I am, though tossed about
with many a conflict, many a doubt;
fightings and fears within, without,
O Lamb of God, I come.

*3 Just as I am, poor, wretched, blind;
sight, riches, healing of the mind,
yea, all I need, in thee to find,
O Lamb of God, I come.

4 Just as I am: thou wilt receive;
wilt welcome, pardon, cleanse, relieve,
because thy promise I believe,
O Lamb of God, I come.

5 Just as I am, thy love unknown
has broken every barrier down;
now to be thine, yea, thine alone,
O Lamb of God, I come.

6 Just as I am, of thy great love
the breadth, length, depth,
  and height to prove,
here for a season, then above:
  O Lamb of God, I come.

Charlotte Elliott (1789-1871)

Take my life, and let it be 707

1 Take my life, and let it be
consecrated, Lord, to thee;
take my moments and my days,
let them flow in ceaseless praise.
Take my hands, and let them move
at the impulse of thy love;
take my heart, it is thine own;
it shall be thy royal throne.

2 Take my voice, and let me sing
always, only, for my King;
take my intellect, and use
every power as thou shalt choose.
Take my will, and make it thine;
it shall be no longer mine.
Take myself, and I will be
ever, only, all for thee.

Francis Ridley Havargal (1836-1879) alt.

Savior, like a shepherd lead us 708

1 Savior, like a shepherd lead us;
much we need thy tender care;
in thy pleasant pastures feed us;
for our use thy folds prepare.
Blessed Jesus!
Thou hast bought us, thine we are.

2 Early let us seek thy favor,
early let us learn thy will;
do thou, Lord, our only Savior,
with thy love our bosoms fill.
Blessed Jesus!
Thou hast loved us: love us still.

Dorothy Ann Thrupp, *Hymns for the Young,* ca. 1830, alt.

My country, 'tis of thee 717

1 My country, 'tis of thee,
sweet land of liberty,
of thee I sing;
land where my fathers died,
land of the pilgrim's pride,
from every mountain side
let freedom ring.

2 My native country, thee,
land of the noble free,
thy name I love;
I love thy rocks and rills,
thy woods and templed hills;
my heart with rapture thrills
like that above.

3 Let music swell the breeze,
and ring from all the trees
sweet freedom's song;
let mortal tongues awake,
let all that breathe partake,
let rocks their silence break,
the sound prolong.

4 Our fathers' God, to thee,
author of liberty,
to thee we sing;
long may our land be bright
with freedom's holy light;
protect us by thy might,
great God, our King.

Samuel Francis Smith (1808-1895)

God of our fathers 718

1 God of our fathers, whose almighty hand
leads forth in beauty all the starry band
of shining worlds
   in splendor through the skies,
our grateful songs before thy throne arise.

2 Thy love divine hath led us in the past,
in this free land by thee our lot is cast;
be thou our ruler,
   guardian, guide, and stay
thy word our law,
   thy paths our chosen way.

3 From war's alarms,
   from deadly pestilence,
be thy strong arm our ever sure defense;
thy true religion in our hearts increase,
thy bounteous goodness
   nourish us in peace.

4 Refresh thy people on their toilsome way,
lead us from night to never-ending day;
fill all our lives with love and grace divine,
and glory, laud, and praise be ever thine.

Daniel Crane Roberts (1841-1907)

O beautiful for spacious skies 719

1 O beautiful for spacious skies,
for amber waves of grain,
for purple mountain majesties
above the fruited plain!
America! America!
God shed his grace on thee,
and crown thy good with brotherhood
from sea to shining sea.

2 O beautiful for heroes proved
in liberating strife,
who more than self their country loved,
and mercy more than life!
America! America!
God mend thine every flaw,
confirm thy soul in self-control,
thy liberty in law.

3 O beautiful for patriot dream
that sees beyond the years
thine alabaster cities gleam,
undimmed by human tears!
America! America!
God shed his grace on thee,
and crown thy good with brotherhood
from sea to shining sea.

Katherine Lee Bates (1859-1929), alt.

O say can you see 720

1 O say can you see,
by the dawn's early light,
what so proudly we hailed
at the twilight's last gleaming,
whose broad stripes and bright stars,
through the perilous fight,
o'er the ramparts we watched,
were so gallantly streaming?
And the rockets' red glare,
the bombs bursting in air,
gave proof through the night
that our flag was still there.
O say does that star-spangled
banner yet wave
o'er the land of the free
and the home of the brave?

Francis Scott Key (1779-1843)

Index Of First Lines